AUTOMOTIVE
PARTS SALES 101

Other Books By Tim Northburg

Automotive Sales Books:

AUTOMOTIVE SALES PLAYBOOK

AUTOMOTIVE SALES 101

KNIGHTS OF THE BLACKTOP

AUTOMOTIVE SALES PHONE MASTERY

AUTOMOTIVE INTERNET SALES MASTERY

AUTOMOTIVE DATA MINING 101

Motivational Books:

DECIDE ON IT!

FUEL THE FURNACE

FUEL THE FURNACE WORKBOOK

OTTEROCITY!

OTTEROCITY! FIELD GUIDE

REALIZE IT!

REALIZE IT! GOALS WORKBOOK

SALES IS MASHED POTATOES

AUTOMOTIVE PARTS SALES 101

Basic Principles of Selling Parts and Accessories

Tim Northburg

ISBN: 1502521393

ISBN-13: 978-1502521392

CONTENTS

PROLOGUE

In dealerships today, we focus a majority of our efforts on Sales and Service. In sales, we want to increase our sold numbers. In our service drive we want to increase RO's, customer pay. Either way, we want to retain as many customers as possible.

What about the Parts Department? They are just as important to the well-being of the dealership as the sales and service departments. Having properly trained and effective parts personnel is the first key to selling more parts and accessories. The second key is having a process in place within the dealership that helps spread awareness that you sell additional parts and accessories.

So, why sell more parts and accessories?

There are many reasons. First, it makes your manufacturer happy. If nothing else, you want your factory rep to be happy with your parts and accessories numbers. Second, it helps retain customers to the dealership. In fact, millions of dollars are spent at secondary parts and accessories stores every day. More often than not, customers purchase wiper blades, floor mats, batteries, tires, side-step bars, roof racks and such outside of the dealer because they simply were not asked at the dealership. In addition, the customer believes they can get a better price elsewhere.

There are some techniques and processes you can put into place to help correct that issue and gain those parts and accessories sales at your dealership.

What are you doing daily, in your parts department, to increase your parts and accessories sales? More often than not, all you have to do is ask for the sale.

Introduction

Parts is Parts—right? Parts sell themselves. A vehicle breaks down, a service advisor suggests work, the customer accepts to do the work, and a part is sold. It is that simple.

Not always. If you live by the service drive, you also die by the service drive. What happens if your service drive slows down, for whatever reason? Where are your parts sales then? Why do you have obsolescent parts sitting on your shelf unsold? Why is the manufacturer screaming at you to sell more parts and accessories?

I know that parts turn and obsolescence is every Parts Manager's nightmare. However, are you focusing every effort in handling every parts opportunity? Is your sales department helping drive accessory sales? Are your service advisors working to help push parts and accessories that you need to sell?

The thing about parts and accessories sales is that the majority of them don't have huge markups. It takes a whole lot of parts sales to make a healthy profit.

My General Manager had a philosophy about selling—and it applies to anything you might sell; cars, service, parts, you name it His philosophy was: Sales is Mashed Potatoes. (Potatoes = profit.) Sometimes you get a big potato. Sometimes you get a medium or small potato. Many times, you get a tiny, itty-bitty potato. At the end of the month, you take all your potatoes and put them in a pot, boil them, mash them up, and you have a whole lot of mashed potatoes. You forget about the size of the potatoes. They all contributed to the big pot of mashed potatoes. *Sales is Mashed Potatoes* is another book I wrote if you want to check it out. However, the philosophy applies here.

Parts sales is the same way. You have to sell as many parts and accessories as you can, from anywhere you can. If you can do this, it will

1

add up to a whole lot of sales and you will be profitable at the end of the month.

In *Automotive Parts Sales 101* we will distill some basic principles that will help you and your parts personnel thrive and sell more parts and accessories, both to internal and external customers. This book will help you turn opportunities into parts and accessory sales. You will learn how to properly handle and convert your parts calls and effectively correspond with online parts customers. Most importantly, it will help focus your energy on building a culture of parts and accessory sales within your dealership.

Now, go out there and sell a lot of parts!

The Parts Counter

Not Just Pieces Parts

THE DREADED PARTS COUNTER

Put yourself in the customer's shoes for a moment . . .

You walk up to the parts counter. The parts person is on the phone with another customer/dealer looking up a part. You stand there for five minutes while the person on the phone avoids eye contact and searches the online catalog for a part. Then as soon as they get off the phone, they turn and hand a part to the service tech that walked up to the counter moments after you. Finally, they turn to you and ask, "How can I help you?" in an annoyed tone.

This may not happen in every dealership but this is going on every day in dealerships across the country.

Why?

Maybe it is because the parts person is having a bad day. Maybe because the parts department isn't held to the same customer service standards as the rest of the dealership. Or, maybe it is because of training or care.

You may say, "This does not happen in our dealership."

I say, great! However, have you snuck back to your parts counter and watched what really happens on a daily basis with every customer? Nobody is perfect.

The main question to ask yourself is; Do we have a culture of customer care in our parts department?

THE MEET AND GREET

Sometimes, all that is needed is for the parts advisor to make eye contact and acknowledge the customer waiting. It can be that simple. Many times we get into our daily routine and forget something as simple as this.

In addition, the parts advisor can whisper to the customer waiting.

PARTS ASSOCIATE: "I will be with you in a moment."

This puts the customer at ease knowing they are acknowledged and will be helped in a moment.

REMEMBER: There is nothing worse than standing somewhere waiting for help, ignored by the staff.

BUILDING RAPPORT

As in any customer service-related position, when dealing with customers, it is good to build rapport quickly. This needs to be done in a natural and open manner.

WAYS TO BUILD RAPPORT:

- Match and Mirror.
- Use Tonality.

MATCHING AND MIRRORING: Match their body language. If your customer is leaning in, then lean in a little bit. If they are folding their hands, then fold your hands. Match their pace of speech. If they are talking fast, the speed up your talk a bit. If they are talking slow, then slow down a bit.

TONALITY: If you want someone to listen to you, soften your voice slightly. Don't raise your voice. Be excited, and sound excited, but don't sound phony.

IS IT IN STOCK?

All customers want to know if you have the part in stock. Now, not all need the part immediately. Nor, do they know that you might be able to get the part overnight or within a few days.

CUSTOMER: "Do you have XYZ part in stock?"

PARTS ASSOCIATE: "Let me check the availability of that part . . . is that something you need immediately?"

                        "If we had to order it in, can you wait a day or two for it?"

Act like a politician; throw a question back at the customer. It is important to find out if the customer really needs it "right now" or may be willing to wait for you to get the part in.

DO NOT TELL THEM IT IS NOT AVAILABLE!

AVAILABILITY

If you look up the part and you don't have it in stock, the worst thing you can say is, "No, that is not in stock." Your customer will be on to the next parts department/store to find that part.

There are only two answers to the question; "Do you have it in stock?"

PARTS ASSOCIATE: "I have it here, available now . . ."

-or-

"I can get it here for you by X . . ."

Only use one of these two!

REMEMBER: Don't say you do not have it in stock!

UP SELLING

When someone is asking about a specific part/accessory think of a related part/accessory that goes with it and ask if they need it or suggest that they get that too.

It might be wise to have your parts team do this exercise: On a piece of paper write out what parts are most commonly asked for, and what related parts go with it. They may already know this, but it is good top of mind awareness to write it out and have it posted at the counter as a good reminder.

What kind of parts are the most commonly asked for:

Part   Related parts to Suggest

Accessory   Related Accessory to Suggest

GO FOR THE UP SELL!

You won't get it, if you don't ask for it. Sometimes all you need to do is ask/suggest other parts or accessories and the customer will buy them.

Consistency is the key to up selling. Always ask/suggest something with their order:

PARTS ASSOCIATE: "Are there any other accessories you need for your vehicle?"

Winter: "Do you need any all season mats?"

"Would you like to change your wiper blades at this time?"

"How are your tires doing?"

"How about some side step bars to go with your roof rack/rails? It will help you load things on top."

"Would you like to buy any key chains or hats?"

Always be thinking of other things to suggest.

PARTS PHONE UP

How do you sell parts over the phone?

THE PARTS CALL

Just like a customer calling the sales department asking about a vehicle, a parts customer calling about a part is a highly important call. Treat every call as if it is a "HOT" customer.

- Be prepared to take a call at all times.
- Clock it mentally to zero and clear your head before you pick up the phone.

THE PARTS CALL:

1. HAVE A GOOD INTRODUCTION:

PARTS ASSOCIATE: "Thanks for calling (DEALER) Parts, this is (YOUR NAME) can I help you?"

CUSTOMER: "I am looking for XYZ part/accessory . . . Is it available? How much?

PARTS ASSOCIATE: "I am familiar with that part it will take me a minute to look it up/get that price . . . In case we get cut off, your # is? Your last name is spelled? Your first name is?

"Great, give me a quick moment to look that up for you."

2. ASK QUESTIONS:

Think about the related parts/accessories from before. Either on the counter or over the phone it is good to ask questions pertaining to the part/assessor they are enquiring about.

PARTS ASSOCIATE: "Will you be needing . . . oil, fluid, filter, belt, etc with that?"

12

THE PARTS CALL CONTINUED

3. GIVE THEM THE AVAILABILITY:

Remember don't say you don't have it in stock!

PARTS ASSOCIATE: "I have it here, available now . . ."

"I can get it here for you by X . . ."

4. TELL THEM THE PRICE:

Tell the customer the price and be ready for their answer. Customers always think the price is too high.

PARTS ASSOCIATE: "The price of that part is X!"

"I have a few choices for you, I have this part for X$ or that part for X$ . . . which one works best for you?"

5. FEATURES AND BENEFITS

CUSTOMER: "I can get it cheaper elsewhere."

PARTS ASSOCIATE: "That may be true, keep in mind, you can always get a cheaper part for lesser quality and reliability."

When talking about parts give your customer a reason why they should buy the part from you.

- OEM / Genuine parts
- Quality
- Service
- Warranty
- Always here to service you / X years in business.
- Stand behind our parts.

THE PARTS CALL CONTINUED

6. GO FOR THE CLOSE

You don't get a sale without closing first!

ASSUMPTIVE CLOSES:

PARTS ASSOCIATE: "Which one works best for you?"

"That will work for you, won't it?"

"Shall we give that one a try?"

"Can I get that ordered for you?"

"When would you like to get that installed?"

"When would you like to come pick that up?"

"I can take a credit card and have it waiting for you, your card number is?"

7. HANDLE OBJECTIONS:

Now, the customer is going react one of three ways and you have to be ready to handle them. (We will cover how to handle objections in another chapter.)

1. ACCEPTANCE: They will give you a credit card, or come down and get it.

2. HESITATION: They will react in a way that you will need to notice. They may have a hesitation or pause on the phone. Usually this is all about the price and they will be thinking they need to shop around for a cheaper price.

3. IMPATIENCE: They may be abrupt and want to hang up. You will need to keep them on the phone and find a way to get the part quick for them or you will lose them due to their impatience.

ONLINE PARTS SALES

How do you sell virtual parts and accessories?

ONLINE PARTS SALES

Many dealerships have online parts order forms. Other dealerships have an online parts and accessory catalogue where customers can shop, and buy parts right from the web page or special website.

How do you handle your parts orders? Do you designate one person to handle all of your online inquiries or live chat? Or, does your entire parts team handle and respond to your parts emails, live chats, and orders?

Whatever you choose, your online parts customers need to be handled in a timely, efficient manner. They are just as important as your walk up customer, or phone in customer.

Yes, you might get a lot of people asking stupid questions, or not replying to your email response, but you need to treat every opportunity as a chance to sell a part or accessory. Do you best in responding fast, and professionally.

ONLINE ORDER RESPONSE

If you have an online catalogue where customers can buy online this is a good response to their purchase order.

Dear (CUSTOMER FULL NAME),

My name is (NAME) and I am your (DEALER) Parts Associate working on your online order.

We received your parts/accessory order and I will be processing it personally.

To confirm, you purchased; (PARTS/ACCESSORIES ORDERED)

I will be in contact with you to confirm the parts are in, and I will notify you when they have been shipped.

If you have any questions, you can call me at (PARTS PHONE #).

Thank You,

(PARTS ASSOCIATE SIGNATURE)

ONLINE PARTS REQUEST

If you have an online parts/accessory request form, customers will fill that out asking you availability of that part/accessory. Use this template to reply to their request.

Dear (CUSTOMER FULL NAME),

My name is (YOUR NAME) and I am your (DEALER) Parts Associate working on your online request.

We received your parts/accessory request. I am working to check the availability and or price.

To confirm, you requested; (PARTS/ACCESSORIES REQUESTED)

Are you wanting us to install it, or is that something you are going to do yourself?

I will be in contact with you shortly to confirm the parts are in, and I will answer any questions you may have.

Should you need to get a hold of me immediately, you can call me at (PARTS PHONE #).

Thank You,

(PARTS ASSOCIATE SIGNATURE)

ONLINE PARTS REQUEST MESSAGE

The following messages will increase your chance of your customer calling you back so you can talk more about the parts/accessories they requested.

PARTS ASSOCIATE: "Hi this is (NAME) Parts Specialist from (DEALER)…"

TELL THEM WHY YOU ARE CALLING:

VIP SPECIALIST: "I am calling to confirm the part/accessory that you inquired about online and to see if you have any further questions and if this is the only part/accessory that you need at this time."

FINISH THE MESSAGE:

VIP SPECIALIST: "If we happen to miss each other I'll call you back tomorrow/later. Thank You."

ONLINE PARTS CALL

The primary purpose of this call is to get the customer to come in and puy your part/accessory.

VIP SPECIALIST:	"Hello, this is (NAME) VIP Specialist from (DEALER), is this a good time?"
CUSTOMER:	"Yes."
PARTS ASSOCIATE:	"I am calling regarding your part/accessory request online?"
CUSTOMER:	"Great."
PARTS ASSOCIATE:	"To confirm, you were wanting to know the availability/price of (PART/ACCESSORY), Is that correct?"
CUSTOMER:	"Yes."
PARTS ASSOCIATE:	"Now, are there any other parts/accessories that you will need in addition to that that you would like me to check on as well at this time?" (Here is where you may want to suggest additional like parts/accessories.)

IF THEY NEED ADDITIONAL PARTS/ACCESSORIES:

CUSTOMER:	"Yes, I also need . . ."
PARTS ASSOCIATE:	"Great, let me check on that as well."

IF THEY ONLY WANT PARTS/ACCESSORIES REQUESTED

CUSTOMER:	"No, just that."
PARTS ASSOCIATE:	"Okay, I will check on the availability of that for you right now.

ONLINE PARTS CALL CONTINUED

PARTS ASSOCIATE: "I have it here, available now . . ."

-or-

"I can get it here for you by X . . ."

GO FOR THE ORDER:

PARTS ASSOCIATE: "When would you like to come pick that up?"

-or-

"Can I get that ordered for you?"

IF THEY WANT TO KNOW THE COST:

CUSTOMER: "How much is it?"

PARTS ASSOCIATE: "It is ($X) if you get it installed here. Or, ($X) for the part only and you install it yourself."

ASSUMPTIVE CLOSES:

PARTS ASSOCIATE: "When would you like to get that installed?"

"I can take a credit card and have it waiting for you, your card number is?"

ONLINE PARTS CONFIRMATION IN STOCK

Use this template to reply to confirm the parts request and to arrange payment and shipping.

Dear (CUSTOMER FULL NAME),

My name is (YOUR NAME) and I am your (DEALER) Parts Associate working on your online request.

The parts you requested are in stock. The total price is ($X) and, if you wish, I can have them installed for (INSTALLED PRICE).

To confirm, you requested; (PARTS/ACCESSORIES)

I can take a credit card number and have your parts available for pick up. Or, I can ship them directly to you.

Let me know as soon as possible, what you would like to do.

Should you need to get a hold of me immediately, you can call me at (PARTS PHONE #).

Thank You,

(PARTS ASSOCIATE SIGNATURE)

LIVE CHAT

There are people who will not walk-in, fill out a form online, e-mail, or call into the dealer. Live chat is becoming a more predominant way to engage with customers. With busy lifestyles, laptops, smart phones, and smart pads, connectivity is at our customer's fingertips wherever they go. Customers are engaging in live chat during work, at lunch or coffee breaks, or while they are waiting somewhere. (For example: picking up the kids, soccer practice, dance lessons, at the doctor's office, etc.)

Live chat provides a quick way to get the information they want. It allows them to do this anonymously without having to fill out a form or give out their email. (That is tough on us!)

Live chat is a great tool if used properly. It gives us another lead to work. Live chat can be more difficult because of the anonymity the customer has. They don't have to give you any of their information if they don't want to and they expect you to answer their questions, right there and then. Like any tool, it can work against you if used incorrectly.

REMEMBER: **Do your best! Engage the customer—give information and you will get information.**

CHAT PROCESS

Like everything you do, you should have a process. Here is a basic process for a parts live chat. The steps may or may not go in this exact order and there may be others to add. It is important to outline the basic steps that should be incorporated into your live chat process and consistently follow it.

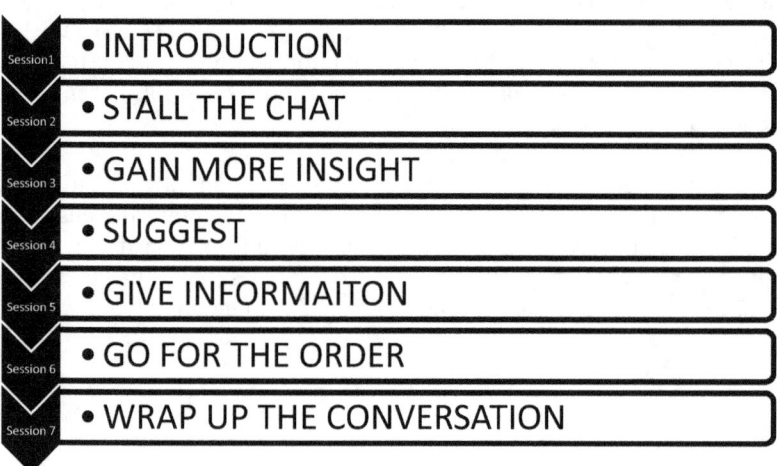

REMEMBER: A good process allows you to get back on track when customers throw you "curve balls!"

SESSION 1 - INTRODUCTION

THE INTRODUCTION

There are a few trains of thought here in the introduction. The first one is to respond in a way that you get their name up front. The other one is to ask once you break the ice and open up the chat. Whatever your dealership decides, make sure you ask somewhere for their name and information. If you don't ask, you don't get, and the chat is a wasted effort.

ONE: Introduce yourself asking for their name.

PARTS ASSOCIATE: "Hello. Thank you for contacting (DEALER) parts department. My name is (FIRST) (LAST), may I ask yours?

You are asking politely here, and by mentioning your *first* and *last name*, you are more likely to get their *first* and *last name*—but not always. That is all right if you don't, you can always try to get it later in the conversation.

TWO: Try to get their phone number.

CUSTOMER: "My name is Bob Jones."

PARTS ASSOCIATE: "Thank you. In case we get cut off is there a number I can reach you at?"

"Or, if you prefer email, do you have an email you would like to share?"

SESSION 2 – STALL THE CHAT

THE QUESTIONS ASKED:

More often than not, the customer opens the chat with an immediate question. Again, slow down, read their question and let them know that you are looking up the answer to their question.

CUSTOMER: "How much is a battery?"
"Do you carry tires?"
"Is XYZ part available?"
"Do you sell XYZ Accessory?"
"How much is XYZ part?"

PARTS ASSOCIATE: "That is a good question, please give me a quick moment to look that up and check our availability/cost."

SESSION 3 – GAIN INSIGHT

While you are looking up parts availability or cost ask a few questions to gain insight as to why they need that part/accessory, of if there are additional parts/accessories needed. Here are a few choices of questions you can ask to open the door to other possibilities.

PARTS ASSOCIATE: "Are there any other parts needed to complete your job?"

"What are you going to use your roof rack for?"

"What are you going to use your tow hitch for?"

"How many miles do you usually put on your tires?"

"Would you like the lowest, average, or best tire?"

"Are there any tire brands you prefer?"

"Have you thought about having us install the (PART/ACCESSORY) for you?"

"Would you like the average, or best battery?"

REMEMBER: If you automatically tell them the part/accessory availability or price then you don't have a shot of up-selling them or getting the order.

SESSION 4 - SUGGEST

If you sense the customer is being agreeable with you then you might want to suggest additional parts and accessories to go with the parts/accessories they are inquiring about online.

PARTS ASSOCIATE: "Have you thought about replacing the (PART) at the same time?"

"Are there any other accessories you need for your vehicle?"

Winter: "Do you need any all season mats?"

"Would you like to change your wiper blades at this time?"

"How are your tires doing?"

"How about some side step bars to go with your roof rack/rails? I will help you load things."

"Would you like to buy any key chains or hats?"

REMEMBER: Only ask questions if you think the customer will go along with the questioning. Gauge their reaction to the questions and determine if you should continue to ask more.

SESSION 5 – GIVE INFORMATION

Create excitement about the part or accessory.

AVAILABILITY:

PARTS ASSOCIATE: "I have it here, available now . . ."

-or-

"I can get it here for you by (DAY) . . ."

Remember don't say you don't have it in stock!

PRICE:

PARTS ASSOCIATE: "The price of that part is ($X)."

-or-

"I have a few choices for you, I have this part for ($X) or that part for ($X) . . . which one works best for you?"

-or-

"It is ($X) if you get it installed here. Or, ($X) for the part only and you install it yourself."

SESSION 6 – GO FOR THE ORDER

Ask them to buy. Many times, sales are lost because you don't ask for the sale. It is all right to ask them to do business with you.

PARTS ASSOCIATE: "When would you like to get that installed, today or tomorrow?"

-or-

"I can take a credit card and have it waiting for you, your card number is? When would you like to pick it up?"

-or-

"I can take a credit card and ship it directly to you, your card number is and your address is?"

SESSION 7 – WRAP-UP CONVERSATION

Summarize the discussion and any action points. This tells the customer that you were listening to everything they said during the live chat.

PARTS ASSOCIATE: "To summarize things, you are looking for (PART/ACCESSORY) which is in stock right now and you would like to come down and have it installed/pick it up on (DAY)."

Ask if there is anything else they need.

PARTS ASSOCIATE: "Is there anything else I can help you with?"

In part of your wrap up, give them your hours, directions, and contact information.

HOURS:

PARTS ASSOCIATE: "Our Parts hours are (TIME)"

CONTACT INFORMATION:

PARTS ASSOCIATE: "Our phone number is (PHONE #). You can call me or I will call you if you prefer."

LOCATION:

PARTS ASSOCIATE: "The Parts Dept. is located (DIRECTIONS)."

FINISH CHAT:

PARTS ASSOCIATE: "Thanks for your time. I will see you (DAY)."

-or-

"I will ship you your part (DAY)."

31

NOT DONE YET!

Just because the chat is finished, does not mean you are done. Most chat tools allow you to forward the transcript to your follow-up system or print it out.

This is a lead!

DON'T FORGET!

If you have their information in the chat, you will be able to continue prospecting that customer and follow-up if you did not get the part or accessory order. Just because the chat is done, does not mean your process is complete. Call or e-mail until they buy or tell you to get lost!

KEEP WORKING THE CUSTOMER!

INTERNAL ACCESSORIES SALES

Expand your sales force!

SALES ACCESSORIES

Like anything, you need to have full buy-in to the goal. If the goal is to sell more parts internally to your sales customers, then your entire sales team including the managers needs to have full buy-in. They need to be 100% committed to pitching and adding accessories at the time of sale.

W.I.I.F.M.:

What's in it for me?

Everyone asks that question. Not everyone will sell accessories simply because it is good for the dealer or organization. (It would be nice, but that is not reality.) People need a reason to sell accessories to their customers, and some of those reasons need to benefit the person selling it for them to actually do it.

REASON #1:

CUSTOMERS CAN EASILY ADD IT TO FINANCE/LEASE: When the salespeople ask at the time of sale, it is easier to roll it into their finance or lease payments rather than bank on the fact that the customer will come back and pay cash at the parts counter.

REASON #2

IT ADDS GROSS TO YOUR DEAL: Some dealerships are set up where the retail price gets charged to the customer, but the internal cost gets charged to the deal, and the profit is rolled to the front-end gross. This way, the sales managers and sales personnel (who are typically paid off gross profit) will be more interested in getting the customer to accessorize their vehicle at the time of the sale.

REASON #3

WE WILL SPIFF YOU: If your dealership does not put the profit into the deal or your sales managers and salespeople are paid flats or mini's, then you might want to consider a spiff program for accessories added to the sale. (One idea is to spiff %5 of the total accessory amount added to the deal once the R.O. is closed and the accessories are billed out.) This will increase the likelihood that the sales staff will sell accessories to their customers.

MAKE IT EASY

You have to make selling accessories easy for the sales team. If it is hard to get accessory information, pricing, or the parts installed in a timely fashion, then your program will fail.

ACCESSORY DISPLAY: Make sure the accessories you want to sell are visible to the customer. Set up a display of some kind to show your wares and make it easy for salespeople to show customers what they look like. You may also want to consider pre-installing accessories on your showroom vehicles.

ACCESSORY BOOKS: Many manufacturers have accessory books that show what accessory goes with what model. Make sure your sales team and managers have enough accessory books to show customers.

ACCESSORY PRICING: There is nothing worse than a customer, who wants to purchase an accessory, and the sales team does not know what the retail price and cost is. (More often than not, this happens when the parts department is closed and sales is left scrambling.) Make sure your sales managers have an up to date cost sheets with cost, retail price and installed price.

ACCESSORY INSTALLATION: Make sure you have people and processes in place for a smooth installation of sold accessories. There is nothing worse for a customer to have to wait eons to get their accessories installed. You may want to have a dedicated service advisor or scheduler that handles all accessory we-owe's. That way they can order the parts, and coordinate installation with the customer and nothing drops through the cracks. Also, have a dedicated team of technicians who handle the installation of said accessories. If it is smooth for the customer and very little heat for the sales team, they will want to sell more accessories.

ACCESSORY PARTS TEAM: Make sure your parts personnel understand that when a salesperson walks up to the counter, they are just as important as a customer. That salesperson may be representing a customer sitting in the showroom, wanting to buy something for their vehicle. Internal customer service is important to selling more parts and accessories. It is also imperative that your parts team knows your accessory inventory and is knowledgeable about what goes on what vehicle.

PRE-INSTALLED ACCESSORIES

Many dealers pre-install accessories on their vehicles. Some install mudguards, wheel locks, spoilers, window tint, clear nose masks, etc. on all of the vehicles on their lot. Others install accessories only on their showroom vehicles. This is a good way to sell additional accessories to the customer.

However, not all customers want that stuff on their vehicles. If the sales team keeps having to "eat the cost" of those pre-installed accessories it can breed contempt between the sales and parts department. Keep in mind, many salespeople and managers are paid off gross profit. If they have to "throw in" unwanted accessories it can take hundreds of dollars out of their gross profit on each deal they do that on, but the parts team gets their sale on the accessories anyway. If this happens a lot, then the sales team won't want to help out anymore.

Talk with your sales team. Communicate. Make sure you have a process in place of being able to swap accessories that are movable to other vehicles if the customer does not want them. Also, decide as a team what if you want to accessorize showroom vehicles or the entire lot. Everyone has to be committed to the plan for it to succeed.

ACCESSORY SPECIALIST

Some stores have an accessory specialist that meets with the customer after the sale, but before they go into the finance office to complete the paperwork. This specialist offers every customer the option to accessorize their vehicle and tries to sell them undercoating, LoJack, and other items. It can be an additional profit center for the dealership, and it ensures that every customer is asked to purchase accessories.

OBJECTIONS

How do you overcome them?

WHY DO PEOPLE OBJECT?

When dealing with objections it is important to understand why people object. Earlier I mentioned the three outcomes of asking for the parts order. You have to recognize the final two with your customers in order to understand their objection and close the sale.

THREE OUTCOMES:

1. ACCEPTANCE: They will give you a credit card number to hold the part or come right down and get it.

2. HESITATION: Most customers are budget conscious and they believe that the dealership charges excessively for parts. Many times, they won't come out and tell you this. They will react in a way that you will need to notice. They may have a hesitation or pause on the phone. Usually this is all about the price and they will be thinking they need to shop around for a cheaper price.

3. IMPATIENCE: The customer may need the part immediately to fix their vehicle. They may be abrupt and want to hang up. You will need to keep them on the phone and find a way to get the part quick for them or you will lose them due to their impatience.

THE CUSTOMER REACTION

When someone objects it is usually because of price, or they don't see the value. Don't take it personal, they are not objecting to you. Take a deep breath and relax!

Listen to customer's reply:

CUSTOMER: "Oh, okay."

                    -or-

                    "Really that much?"

                    -or-

                    "That is a little high."

                    -or-

                    "Oh, you don't have it now?"

                    -or-

                    "That long eh?"

Clue in on these phrases, as they are an indication that the customer may go shop elsewhere.

THE I.I.R.T TECHNIQUE

Listen with the intent to understand and be empathetic. When you "Listen" to your customer's objections, they think you are really concerned with them. This will strengthen your relationship and build up more trust. Don't take the objection personally. Remember the nature of the customer is to "get out" when they feel uncomfortable. This process must happen to get to the "close."

IDENTIFY with the customer. This makes them feel that you are listening to them. It puts you in the seat of empathy and builds up deposits.

- "I understand how you feel many of my customers have felt the same thing…"

ISOLATE the objection. Figure out their real concern and if that is the only thing keeping them from moving forward.

- "Other than…"
- "Is there anything else…"

REFINE the objection. Ask open-ended questions targeted at the objection to gain clarity and insight as to the strength and validity of the objection. This further questioning builds your angle to head off or overcome the objection. Then use logic and support it with appropriate information addressing the concern.

- "Many of my customers have found…"
- "What is it about the price you don't like?"
- "How soon do you really need the part?

TARGET the objection. Summarize and answer the objection logically. Provide options that move toward a purchase decision and close the deal.

- **"I don't know if they would . . . if I could do X . . . would you buy our part right now?"**

OBJECTION: "The part costs too much!"

IDENTIFY

"I understand how you feel, the cost of arts/accessories/tires/batteries/etc. keep going up and up."

ISOLATE

"Other than the cost being a little too much, is there anything else keeping you from buying our part/accessory?"

REFINE

- "Have you received any other prices?"
- "Are you pricing genuine parts, 3rd party parts from a parts store, or used parts?"
- "How much less are they quoting you?"
- "Sometimes you have to pay a little more for better quality . . ."
- "Do you want to go with the genuine part?"
- "What price were you hoping for?"

Keep them from hanging up, or walking away!!!!

CLOSE

TARGET

PARTS ASSOCIATE: "Wait a minute, I might have an idea."

(Look up your cost on the part.)

PARTS ASSOCIATE: "Ok, let me ask you a question? If I could do X would you buy our part/accessory?"

X =
- Shave a little off the price.
- Give you a break on installation.
- Get you a 10% discount
- Throw in a keychain/hat.

OBJECTION: "I need that part right now!"

IDENTIFY

"I understand you probably need to get that part immediately to get your vehicle working."

ISOLATE

"Is that the only thing that is keeping you from ordering our part?"

REFINE

- "Could you do without it for 24 hours?
- "Would you consider a non OEM, or a used one?

Keep them from hanging up, or walking away!!!!

CLOSE

TARGET

PARTS ASSOCIATE: "Wait a minute, I might have an idea . . ."

"If you were flexible, and I could have our parts driver run and get it (at another dealer/parts store) and get it here by this afternoon would you buy our part/accessory?"

-or-

"If you were flexible, and I could overnight it and get it here by tomorrow would you buy our part/accessory?"

-or-

"If you were flexible, and I could special order it and get it here in the next few days would you buy our part/accessory?"

LAST DITCH CLOSE

Sometimes when you try to overcome their objection, there is still a sticking point and you don't really know what that is. Use the last ditch close to try to find what it is you are missing, and what it will take to get the order.

PARTS ASSOCIATE: "I would really like to earn your business, what would I have to do to end your shopping with our part/accessory, right now?"

They will usually tell you. You have to decide if it is something, you can or want to do to earn their business.

ABOUT THE AUTHOR

Tim Northburg is an author of multiple sales training and motivational guidebooks. Mr. Northburg started his automotive career in 1996 where he learned highly valuable customer service and needs-based selling skills. In 1998 he gained international experience while managing a Rover, MG, MINI Cooper dealership in Chester, England. Upon returning to America, he spent three years running a Business Development Center where he learned valuable customer follow-up, incoming phone call, prospecting, and owner retention techniques and skills. He spent six years as a Used Car Manager /Desk Manager and is fully trained in, Finance, Marketing, and Public Relations then moved into upper management where he trained, motivated and led a highly successful team of sales professionals. In 2010, he transitioned as the E-Commerce Director managing all internet marketing, including but not limited to, websites, lead sources, social media, SEO, and search marketing while leading a team of internet salespeople to success. Since 2018 he worked as New Car Manager and Used Car Manager roles at the dealership, that he has been at for over 25 years, while continuing to use his knowledge and skills to lead a highly effective sales team. Mr. Northburg's commitment and dedication to the business, his customers, and the salespeople he leads, is evident in his complete training guidebooks. He shares the knowledge gained, throughout his career, because he wants others to succeed as he has.

www.TimNorthburg.com

For More Visit:

www.LifeWorkElements.com

Business. Coaching. Goals. Inspiration.

Motivation. Persistence. Sales. Success. Training.

Elements For Your Life's Work

www.ingramcontent.com/pod-product-compliance
Lightning Source LLC
Chambersburg PA
CBHW051249170526
45165CB00004B/1637